The Rise of
American
Political Parties

Election night, November, 1884, in Printing House Square, New York City. A Democrat, Grover Cleveland, was the winner of the U.S. Presidency, breaking a twenty-four-year winning streak of the Republican party. View is looking down Park Row from the "el" platform at Brooklyn Bridge. (PHOTO BY CUSHING)

◄—A FIRST BOOK—►

The Rise of
American
Political Parties

by Fred J. Cook

FRANKLIN WATTS, INC.
845 Third Avenue, New York, N.Y. 10022

ISBN 0-531-00741-3

  0-531-02362-1 pbk.

Library of Congress Catalog Card Number: 77-161834

Copyright © 1971 by Franklin Watts, Inc.

Printed in the United States of America

4   5

Contents

The "game cocks." Right, Thomas Jefferson, author of the American Declaration of Independence. Left, the brilliant Alexander Hamilton. Both men were instrumental in shaping the philosophy of future American political parties. (PHOTO BY CUSHING)

The Game Cocks– Hamilton and Jefferson

American political parties first began to arise in 1792 when Alexander Hamilton and Thomas Jefferson faced each other "like two fighting cocks," as Jefferson said, across the council table of America's distressed first President, George Washington.

Hamilton and Jefferson were contrasting types, and they represented hostile interests — a conflict in political affairs that has lasted down to the present day.

Hamilton was an aristocrat. Five feet and seven inches tall, boyishly slim, he had a large and handsome head. He dressed in the height of fashion and he carried himself with a military erectness that made him seem taller than he was. A commanding figure, he had high intelligence, great ability — and a deep distrust of the common people and democracy. He favored a king and a royal court, a system patterned after the British monarchy.

Thomas Jefferson was entirely different from Hamilton.

1

More than six feet tall, slender, he seemed angular and loose-jointed. He was careless in his dress, and when he sat, he slouched in whatever position happened to be most comfortable. His clear blue eyes sometimes chilled visitors at first meeting, but on closer acquaintance he could be charming. He was a shy man, a many-sided genius — lawyer, philosopher, planter, inventor. He owned a ten-thousand-acre plantation and had many slaves. This plantation was at Monticello, outside Charlottesville, Virginia, in the foothills of the Blue Ridge Mountains. In Jefferson's youth, this was virtually the American frontier. As a result, Jefferson's sympathies were more with the frontiersmen than with the older tidewater aristocracy, though he could be at home in both societies — or at the Court of France, for that matter. At the core of his beliefs was a passionate faith concerning the "rights of man" about which he had written so eloquently in the Declaration of Independence. Together with this went a conviction that the common people should be allowed to decide their own destiny.

Alexander Hamilton was the Secretary of the Treasury; Thomas Jefferson, the Secretary of State. Washington admired both men. Hamilton had served on his staff during the Revolution and had distinguished himself at Yorktown. Jefferson was a fellow Virginian and former governor of that state. Washington had wanted both men in his Cabinet and had hoped to make the best use of their high talents. He could not guess that he had really elected himself a referee in the brawling of these two game cocks.

Washington could not imagine this because none of the Founding Fathers had had any idea that the new nation would

A view of the State House in Philadelphia where the Constitutional Convention met in 1787. (THE METROPOLITAN MUSEUM OF ART)

ever have opposing political parties. When the Constitution of the United States was drafted in Philadelphia during the long hot summer of 1787, political parties did not exist in the infant nation. The closest that America had come to them was in the fevered agitation that had led to the Revolution itself. The patriots then had been known as Whigs; those colonials loyal to the British Crown had been Tories. With the victory of the American patriots in 1783, these distinctions had disappeared.

The struggle over the ratification of the Constitution had drawn some temporary political battle lines. Those who favored the new form of government became known as Federalists; those who generally opposed it were anti-Federalists. But again, with the official ratification of the Constitution in 1789, these factions became less pronounced as time went on. Washington was such a towering figure and was so respected that he gathered around him the leaders of his day in an administration of apparent unity. No one could conceive at the time that this unity would soon be disrupted by basic differences among President Washington's followers, or that this strange new phenomenon known as a political party would presently be born.

To understand the situation, one must realize what the nation was like at the time. In 1790 the 13 original states had a total population of only four million. Ninety-five percent of these people lived on farms or in small villages; only 5 percent lived in what might be called cities. The sparsely settled Eastern seaboard states were still a virtual wilderness; roads were few and very bad. Farms and villages were cut off from one another, and it was this situation that largely determined the nature of politics.

4

Most issues were local ones and they were settled locally. The political leaders of the day were those who earned the respect of their fellow citizens by their character and talents. It was a personalized leadership, far removed from the huge and powerful political machines America was to know later.

The Constitution itself changed this. It established a national government — and a powerful one. This meant that local interests would be affected as never before by decisions made on the national level. It followed that control of this new government was a supreme prize worth fighting for, since its actions affected all — the wealthy merchants of the Eastern seaboard, the rural farmers, the frontiersmen streaming across the Appalachians to settle in Kentucky and Tennessee and in what were to become the states of Ohio, Indiana, and Illinois in the Northwest Territory.

However, actions that favored one group might work against the interests of others, and so each faction needed to make itself known and felt in the conduct of the national administration. Here was the basic, driving need that would soon lead to the creation of political parties. To bring these parties into being, only two things were necessary: sharp disagreement on vital policies and leaders around whom these clashing interests could marshal their forces. The leaders were there — seated across Washington's council table in the persons of Hamilton and Jefferson, each filled with a growing dislike and distrust of the other. And the issues that would set them at each other's throats arose almost as soon as they assumed their offices.

Hamilton Rides Hard

Alexander Hamilton, at age thirty-four, was determined to take over the new government and fashion it in the image of his desires. If he could not have a president with lifelong kingly powers, if he could not have a hereditary nobility, then he was determined to create an aristocracy of wealth — a privileged class that would have a vested interest in upholding the new national government.

Although Hamilton as Secretary of the Treasury was not the ranking member of the Cabinet — an honor reserved for the Secretary of State — he at once seized control of the reins of government. He had scant respect for anyone else, even for Washington himself. He conducted himself as if he were the prime minister of the new administration, and at every Cabinet meeting he lectured Washington and his fellow secretaries in the manner of a profes-

6

The inauguration of President George Washington on the balcony of the old Federal Hall Building, Wall Street, New York City, in 1789. The 1st U.S. President had high hopes for Jefferson and Hamilton and their unique talents in his Cabinet. (PHOTO BY CUSHING)

sor explaining the facts of life to a group of schoolboys. Jefferson, a far milder man, a philosopher given to understanding others' points of view, and by nature anxious to conciliate, could put up with this for just so long. Hamilton's dictatorial manner seldom failed to raise his hackles.

But at the start it did not seem to matter what Jefferson or anyone else thought; it did not seem to matter how many bruised feelings Hamilton left in his wake. So capable, so brilliant, and so commanding was the young Secretary of the Treasury that he drove through Congress program after program in a wave of unbroken success.

It would take some time for the effect of Hamilton's deeds to register with Jefferson and the public, for there were two sides to his financial reforms. One was good; one, bad. Many of Hamilton's measures were vital in building a stable government, but his programs, in the way they were handled, had one indisputable effect — they made the wealthy wealthier, and they tended to cheat the poor.

When the Revolution ended, the nation was bankrupt. The Continental Congress had tried to finance the war by issuing paper money and paper promises to pay later. The states, many of which had raised their own armies and navies, had followed the same procedure. This flood of paper had become virtually worthless. Soldiers who had been paid in it, small merchants and farmers who had accepted it in payment for goods or produce, felt that it was of little good other than to paper their walls.

Hamilton rightly determined that the government could not function unless its credit was restored. To do this, the old paper debts and promises to pay must be made good. Within a month

8

after he took office in 1789, he decided that two steps were essential: the old national debt must be paid off at one hundred cents on the dollar, and the national government must also take over and pay in full the debts which the individual states had incurred in fighting the war.

So far, so good. But Hamilton leaked his plans to his moneyed friends. Soon insiders in New York, Philadelphia, and Boston went into action. They could buy up the seemingly worthless paper scrip for a song from those who did not know what was about to happen; then when Hamilton's program was approved, the government would pay off the new holders at face value. There were million-dollar fortunes to be made.

At first, there was little opposition to the Hamilton program in Congress. Jefferson and James Madison — a man who was looked upon by Jefferson almost as the son he had never had — recognized the need for a sound financial system. But in the House of Representatives, some less-famous Americans — men close to rural and frontier grass roots — saw what was happening and howled in protest.

Soldiers who had fought and bled in the Revolution were being cheated, they cried. Furthermore, many of the cheaters who were going to reap huge profits had been Tories or Tory sympathizers — members of the wealthy classes who were buying up the paper scrip for as little as ten cents on the dollar. Secretary Hamilton's program, these critics shouted, would rob the courageous, the patriotic, the deserving, and it would reward many who had been secret enemies of the country throughout the Revolution.

In those days, there was no telegraph, no rapid means of

9

Alexander Hamilton is depicted here as Secretary of the Treasury in President Washington's Cabinet. (PHOTO BY CUSHING)

communication; and so, when Hamilton's proposals were introduced into Congress, speculators raised all the money they could and began to buy up the paper scrip. One Federalist congressman dispatched two fast sailing ships to the South to fleece Southerners before they could learn what was happening. And, long after Hamilton's program had been approved, it was disclosed that 29 of the 64 members of Congress had themselves been involved in such insider speculations.

The outcry raised by those who had been cheated grew louder and louder, but Hamilton paid no heed. He had little regard for the public, and thus pushed ahead with the final step in his program — the creation of a national bank. The Constitution, of course, provided for no such bank. But Hamilton argued that the Constitution had conferred upon the national government "implied powers," whereby such a bank might be created.

This contention infuriated Jefferson and Madison. They had been steadily driven into opposition to Hamilton, both because his measures favored the special moneyed and merchant classes of the North, and because he treated all who disagreed with such contempt. James Madison, a short man with pipe-stem legs and a paunch, was one of the most intelligent men of his time. He was powerful and logical in argument and carried great weight in Congress.

But not even Madison, with Jefferson masterminding some of his moves, could stop the Hamilton steamroller. The national bank whipped through Congress, but the vote on it was significant. It showed that the nation was being divided along sectional and class lines. Nineteen of the twenty votes in opposition came from the rural South.

The first Bank of the United States building in Philadelphia, created by Hamilton's bank bill. Passage of the bill started the first great debate of "constitutionality," and the development of factions which eventually split into rival political parties in the United States. (CULVER PICTURES)

The passage of Hamilton's bank bill had another far-reaching effect. Washington, who had nearly always sided with Hamilton, was disturbed. He feared the doctrine of "implied powers." Under it, he felt, the federal government could do almost anything it wished to do; there would be no restraint upon it. Accordingly, he held long conferences with Jefferson and Madison, and he finally asked both to put their objections in writing. The indications were that the President was planning to veto the bank bill.

But Hamilton, who could tolerate no opposition, was furious. In the Federalist drawing rooms of Philadelphia, New York, and Boston, a whispering campaign began to tear down the character of the first U.S. President. Ugly and vicious stories were circulated; the meanest motives were attributed to Washington.

In the end, Washington yielded to Hamilton again and signed the bank bill. Jefferson, while disappointed, never stooped to mudslinging as Hamilton had. Although he felt Washington had been wrong, he still praised him as "purely and zealously republican." The bank battle, however, had stretched Jefferson's relations with Hamilton to the breaking point. He was convinced that Hamilton must be stopped.

So the First Congress adjourned in 1791 with Hamilton everywhere triumphant — and with Jefferson writing a stream of letters to friends and correspondents in various states, feeling out the public pulse, taking the first cautious steps toward the building of a two-party system.

Building a Party

At first glance Jefferson's task looked hopeless. Hamilton seemed to have all the aces up his sleeve. He was the hero of men of power. The wealthy and commercial classes, the lawyers and doctors and preachers — all sang his praises. The Chambers of Commerce were in effect Federalist clubs. The press was almost entirely Hamiltonian. And the electoral dice were loaded.

In America, only the more prosperous citizens could vote. Except for Vermont, every state had written into its constitution property qualifications for voters. Those who worked with their hands and who did not possess sufficient wealth were barred from the polls. In New York State, the constitution drawn up by Federalist John Jay was so strict that the great mass of citizens had no say about anything at election time. As a result, in New York City in 1790, only 1,303 male residents out of 13,330 possessed the right to vote.

14

Although few citizens could vote in 1790, Americans were still deeply interested in politics. Here, townspeople discuss the election in Philadelphia.
(THE BETTMANN ARCHIVE)

This theft of the ballot from the great mass of people played directly into the hands of Hamilton and the Federalists. In a nation in which only the more affluent could vote, it seemed that Hamilton need never worry, for these were the classes most favored by his policies and so were the ones who might be expected to stay chained to him by self-interest.

Only a political leader as canny and sensitive as Thomas Jefferson could have seen a chance where there appeared to be no chance. Only Jefferson, sniffing the political winds, could see that all was not secure in the Hamiltonian Federalist world.

The colonial experience with autocratic rule and the rebellion against it had done much to democratize the nation. The great mass of Americans out on the farms and the frontier felt that one man should have equal rights with another; they hated the idea of being ruled by a king or a privileged class. And the Federalists made no secret of the fact that their ideal government would see the few, placed in the saddle for life, ruling over the many.

Then, too, Hamilton's financial measures had stirred up widespread resentment. The little man who felt he had been cheated by speculators began to hate the Federalists. And in every state, Jefferson discovered, there were a few leaders who believed in the principles of democracy and who feared a drift toward authoritarian government.

In Massachusetts, the stronghold of federalism, there was that firebrand and propagandist of the Revolution, Samuel Adams. Siding with him was John Hancock, whose great sprawling signature had been the first on the Declaration of Independence. In Virginia, Jefferson had James Madison, James Monroe, John Taylor, and others. In New York City, workingmen had organized a social club known as the Sons of Tammany. Could such an organization, wholly democratic in spirit, be turned to political purposes? Jefferson saw the possibility that it could.

His idea, as it took form during 1792, was to draw all of these separate leaders and groups together and make them into one national party. Let the local leaders in each state organize and rally their followers, unite on a program to oust the Federalists, and then return the national government to the people. To accomplish all this, Jefferson needed a propagandist; he needed a national newspaper to offset the Federalist press and to carry his message to the uninformed in far-distant, rural areas.

Madison found just the man Jefferson needed — Philip Freneau, "the poet of the Revolution." Freneau had been a classmate of Madison's at Princeton. He had sacrificed his entire fortune to the Revolutionary cause; he had been captured and imprisoned, his health broken in the foul and disease-ridden hold of a British prison ship. When Madison contacted him in 1791, he was making a bare living scribbling for a New York newspaper.

Freneau was persuaded to move to Philadelphia, then the nation's capital. There he established a paper known as the *National Gazette*. Jefferson gave him a job as a clerk in the State Department at a salary of $250 a year, and he and Madison solicited subscribers to the new paper. Freneau, a fiery democrat, wrote with an acid pen, and it was not long before his savage attacks roused the Federalists to fury.

17

A portrait of Philip Freneau, called the poet of the Revolution. Jefferson and Madison persuaded him to turn his acid pen to attacks on Hamilton's Federalist party. (PHOTO BY CUSHING)

Hamilton, the vainest of men, could never stand criticism. As he and Jefferson fought with increasing bitterness in the inner councils of Washington's administration, Hamilton decided that Jefferson was bent on destroying him — and so, he thought, the nation. In May, 1792, he wrote that Madison and Jefferson were heading "a faction decidedly hostile to me and my administration" and that their views were "subversive of the principles of good government and dangerous to the Union, peace, and happiness of the country."

18

Federalist newspapers, taking their cue from Hamilton, saw the Jeffersonian opposition as virtual treason. Wrote one Massachusetts paper: "Of course, there can be but two parties in the country — the friends of order and its foes." In their rage the Federalists began to regret that the first article of the Bill of Rights had guaranteed freedom to the press. They began to express the thought that newspapers were "a vice" and they toyed with the idea of introducing legislation to suppress hostile ones — a policy that ultimately was to wreck the Federalist party.

While the Federalists nursed their injured feelings, the newspaper war raged on. John Fenno, Hamilton's mouthpiece and editor of the *Gazette of the United States*, denounced administration critics as "mad dogs" and "enemies of the government." The attacks would not be so serious, Fenno wrote, if only America had a king, for "a king at the head of a nation to whom all men of property cling . . . is able to crush the first rising against the laws." No confession could have delighted the Jeffersonians more; Freneau hopped upon this admission of secret longing with savage glee.

Hamilton now lost his equanimity, just as he was to do time and again whenever he was attacked. Using the initials "T.L." — a disguise that fooled no one — he wrote a letter to Fenno's paper attacking Jefferson and demanding that Jefferson resign from Washington's Cabinet. This attack by one Cabinet officer upon another quickly became the talk of the capital. Jefferson ignored the letter as beneath his contempt; but Freneau joined battle. He exposed Hamilton as the author of the "T.L." letter and wrote acidly, "The devil rageth when his time is short."

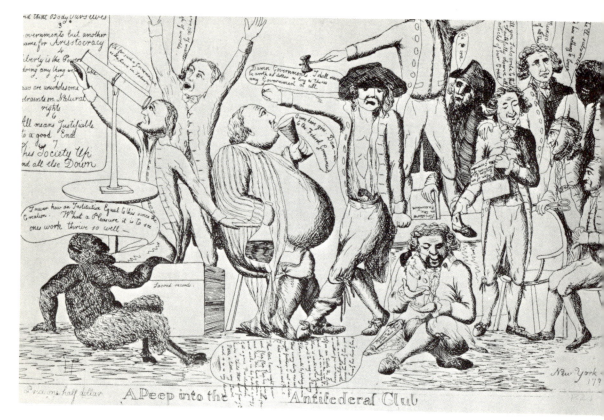

A Federalist cartoon of 1793 captioned "A Peep into the Antifederal Club." It depicts the Jeffersonians as insane people consorting with the devil. Jefferson himself stands on a bench ranting wildly, while the Republican astronomer David Rittenhouse stargazes at left. (NATIONAL ARCHIVES)

Washington still tried to make peace between the two men, but he failed. Jefferson, surrounded by Federalists in the Cabinet, wanted to resign; but the President persuaded him to stay on. In letters to Washington, however, Jefferson made it clear that he felt there could be no compromise with Hamilton because the latter, if not stopped, would destroy the republic and junk the principles for which the Revolution had been fought. Hamilton was a monarchist, Jefferson a democrat; and the future of the nation was at stake in a choice that must be made between the two.

Time and again, Washington overrode Jefferson's request to leave the administration, but by December of 1793, Jefferson could be persuaded no longer. He resigned and returned to his hilltop home at Monticello. The Federalists had their wish. They were no longer to be disturbed by a critic in the councils of government; all power was theirs. And disaster was not far away.

Jefferson Triumphs Over the Federalists

Thomas Jefferson had been the foreign policy expert in the American government, but with Jefferson gone the Federalists assumed full responsibility in that field. Their policies were soon to help work their ruin.

The matter of first importance to the United States was a new treaty with Great Britain. The British had ignored many provisions of the treaty that had ended the Revolutionary War. They still kept their troops in northwest frontier posts around the Great Lakes; they stopped American ships on the high seas, impressed American seamen, and forced them to serve in British warships. They tried to strangle American trade; and, as Jefferson charged, they encouraged the Barbary pirates to prey on American commerce in the Mediterranean.

In an effort to end all this, the Federalists sent Chief Justice

22

of the U.S. John Jay to London in 1794. The British were in a difficult spot. The French Revolution had touched off a war that was to last for decades, and Britain could hardly afford another enemy. However, to England's advantage, Hamilton was pro-British and anti-French. In his friendliness, he told the British ambassador that America had no intention of joining Britain's foes — thus he deprived John Jay in London of much of his bargaining power as an envoy.

The result was what has been called the most shameful treaty this nation ever signed. The British did agree to abandon the frontier posts after June 1, 1796, but that was their only major concession. Most other provisions favored them. Nothing was said about the impressment of American sailors. The Mississippi was opened to British trade, and the West Indies were all but closed to limited American shipping. The treaty amounted to an American alliance with Britain against the ally who had saved Americans in the Revolution — France.

Both Hamilton and Jefferson used the same word in describing the treaty — "execrable." But it was an all-Federalist treaty, and Hamilton had to back it. He determined, however, not to let the public know what the treaty said. An eighteen-day Senate debate was held in secret and behind closed doors, a procedure that would be unthinkable today. And when the treaty was finally ratified in 1795, the Federalist majority in the Senate ordered that it not be published. The public was not to know. At this point, a daring Jeffersonian senator, Stevens Thomas Mason of Virginia, defied the Senate and smuggled a full copy of the treaty to the Jeffersonian press.

23

Jay's Treaty was vastly unpopular in America. Here its author, John Jay, is burned in effigy. (CULVER PICTURES)

With publication of the document, a storm of protest swept the land. Jay's acquiescence to British demands was bad enough, but what really aroused the public to white-hot fury was the way the Federalists had tried to keep the treaty a secret and dupe the nation. Here was proof, in the deed, of Jeffersonian charges that Hamilton and his followers were despots at heart.

Now the Federalists lost the shield behind which they had been sheltered. George Washington decided to retire at the end of his second term, and so the Federalists had to find themselves a new President in 1796. Hamilton did not dare to run. John Jay might have been a candidate, but the Jay treaty had discredited him. In the end, unhappy with the necessity, the Federalists settled on John Adams. While he was vain, crusty, and short-tempered, Adams was nevertheless one of the true political leaders and heroes of the fledgling United States.

The Jeffersonians were not yet strong enough to defeat Adams, but they swept the South and West, with the exception of Maryland. In those days, before the formation of political parties on a formal basis, the President and Vice-President did not run on a single ticket as a team. The man who received the most votes became President; the next, Vice-President. Thus John Adams was elected President and Thomas Jefferson, who held entirely different views, became Vice-President. The Federalists were shocked and horrified. Typical was the remark of one who saw Jefferson as "a formidable evil."

Although Adams was President, Hamilton still ruled the Federalist party and influenced decisions. Adams made the mistake of keeping certain members of Washington's last Cabinet, and these were loyal to Hamilton, not to himself. Since the Hamiltonians were strongly pro-British, it was not long before they were pushing Adams and the nation into a quasi-war with France. Lasting from 1798 to 1800, it was a war fought on the sea, without any formal declaration, but it was a war nonetheless. A small standing army was created, a new navy built. Taxes soared, and the Jeffersonians, urging peace, denounced the administration, the war, and the taxes.

As they so often did when their authority was challenged by what they considered "the rabble," the Federalists reacted with anger, outrage, and repression. They jammed through Congress the Alien and Sedition Acts. The Alien Act gave the President the power to deport any alien whom he thought might be "dangerous" or whom he "suspected" of "treasonable or secret machination against the government." Evidence was not necessary; "suspicion" in the mind of just one man, the President, was enough. The Sedition Act was even worse. This provided for the fine and imprisonment of anyone who dared to criticize official policies. In effect, it wiped out the First Amendment guarantees of freedom of speech and press.

No sooner had these laws been passed than Federalist prosecutors and judges went into action. No real use was ever made of the Alien Act, but the Sedition Act was widely and brutally enforced. No Jeffersonian editor, no man in the street who happened to utter a criticism of John Adams, no congressman who opposed the administration was safe. The instant a mouth was opened or pen was set to paper, it became a certainty that arrest, conviction, and imprisonment would follow.

A congressman from Vermont, Matthew Lyon, became one of the first and most celebrated victims of Federalist prosecution. A Revolutionary War veteran who had been one of Ethan Allen's Green Mountain Boys, Lyon was a hot-tempered democrat and he had so enraged the Federalists that he had been attacked and beaten on the floor of the House of Representatives. But Lyon was not the kind of a man to be muzzled. When the *Rutland Herald* refused to print one of his speeches, he started his own newspaper; he called it *The Scourge of Aristocracy*. Lyon was instantly arrested, railroaded before a Federalist judge, convicted, and fined a thousand dollars. He was also sentenced to four months in prison. There was a fairly decent jail in Rutland, where the trial had been held, but the vicious Federalists wanted nothing decent for Lyon. They packed him off to Vergennes, forty miles away, where there was a hell-hole of a prison. There they threw him into a filthy, narrow cell with little light and no heat.

At this outrage, Vermont erupted. The Green Mountain Boys threatened to tear the jail apart and were kept from doing so only because Lyon pleaded with them to obey the law. Thousands signed petitions asking for Lyon's pardon and release, but President Adams refused even to touch the documents. This arrogant action only fanned the public's rage. Lyon became the hero of Vermont. While still in prison, he was nominated and re-elected to Congress, defeating his Federalist opponent by a margin of almost two to one.

The result rocked the Adams administration and the Federalist party, but the latter could not, or would not, change. The Federalists kept right on throwing critics and Jeffersonian editors

Old print shows a brawl in Congress between Federalist Roger Griswold and Republican Matthew Lyon, 1798. (THE BETTMANN ARCHIVE)

into prison. The reign of terror lasted for more than two years, from the summer of 1798 into the autumn of 1800; and, as brutality piled upon brutality, public fury mounted. This was not the freedom for which men had fought and died in the Revolution.

In reality, the Federalists were doing Jefferson's propaganda work for him, but it took a leader with vision to capitalize

28

on the issues. Jefferson was just such a leader. As the Presidential campaign of 1800 drew near, he gathered his aides about him at the nightly dinner table in Philadelphia's Indian Queen Tavern, and there they mapped out party strategy. The political device known as the party platform had not yet been invented, and so what counted was the stand the Jeffersonians took in Congress. Under Jefferson's guidance, they hammered hard and constantly at the big issues the Federalists had provided them with: the Alien and Sedition Acts, heavy taxes, the burden of a standing army and navy, the "usurious interest" on war loans. They constantly called for freedom of speech and press. Defying the Sedition Act, Jeffersonian congressmen mailed out copies of speeches attacking the administration. The letters blanketed the country, and Adams was driven nearly crazy with them. Unable to throw half of Congress into prison, he was balked; he could find no way to halt the attacks.

While all this was taking place, Jefferson was putting together a national party of his own. He called it the Republican party, but it was as often referred to in the press as the Democratic party, the name it was finally to adopt. Jefferson now had his agents and his party organization in every state. As the campaign raged, he stayed at Monticello, riding over his acres like the least concerned of men, leaving to his lieutenants the task of getting out the vote — and to his enemies the business of committing political suicide.

In this, the Federalists obliged him. They were torn apart. Hamilton had come to hate President Adams so strongly that he began to attack the President of his own party in print. In the chaos that followed, Jefferson emerged the winner, but he did not carry enough states for outright election.

The framers of the Constitution had written into it a curious device that still exists. It is called the Electoral College. Presidents were not to be elected by popular vote, but were to be chosen by a group of electors drawn from each state. Presumably, the electors would vote for the candidate who carried their state, but nothing in the Constitution said they had to. Furthermore, a candidate, in order to win, had to have not just more electoral votes than anyone else but a majority of the vote in the Electoral College. If he did not have such a majority, the House of Representatives would decide who should become President.

This was the first time an election had been thrown into the House. The Federalists, hating Jefferson, tried to gather enough votes to elect Aaron Burr, who had been Jefferson's lieutenant in New York. Burr, however, gave them no help, and in the end the Federalist plotting collapsed.

Thus Thomas Jefferson became President as well as the leader of a new party. And a precedent for a competing, two-party system had been established.

The Virginia Dynasty

Jefferson's victory in 1800 started a long reign of American Presidents from Virginia. For the next twenty-four years, the White House was to be occupied by this Virginia dynasty — Jefferson, James Madison, and James Monroe.

The Federalists, having thoroughly discredited themselves, became a minority party. They remained strong on the local scene in the mercantile world of New England and they retained pockets of strength in other areas — Virginia and Maryland, for example. But as a national party, capable of mounting a strong bid for the Presidency, they were dead.

During the War of 1812, in fact, the Federalists all but committed treason. So unpopular was the war in New England that the Federalists there threatened in 1814 to secede from the union. However, this movement was stopped by the coming of

31

peace and by General Andrew Jackson's great victory over the British in the Battle of New Orleans in 1815. The nation thrilled with pride at Jackson's feat; the general became a national hero, and the Federalists retired grumbling.

In many states the Federalists simply quit. After 1817 in New Hampshire, for example, they did not even run candidates for state offices. The weakness of that party brought a sharp drop in the percentage of voters who went to the polls. In Rhode Island, only 15 percent of the electorate voted in 1819, and in Vermont and Connecticut only slightly more than 20 percent.

This political lopsidedness wrought changes in the party of Jefferson. The "black democrat," whom the wealthier classes had feared, had proved not to be so terrible in the Presidency after all. Indeed, he and his successors, Madison and Monroe, absorbed much of the opposition into the ranks of the Republican party.

Other political changes resulted from the War of 1812. Jefferson had originally believed that democracy could thrive only in an agrarian society in which the great majority of the people could stand independently on their own broad acres. He had opposed manufacturing and the industrialization of society, fearing that this would place overwhelming power in the hands of a small banking and moneyed class. But the war had demonstrated that America would be weak and helpless without factories. The result was ironic, for the party of Jefferson began to adopt the principles of his hated rival, Hamilton.

As early as Washington's administration, Hamilton had prepared a "Report on Manufactures." It drew little comment at that time, but it outlined principles that were later to become the policy of the American nation. Hamilton recommended a protective tariff to encourage the development of American industry. The tariff would favor just the kind of moneyed and industrial classes Jefferson feared, but Hamilton had offered a bone to the farming interests. Revenue from the tariff would be used for "internal development" — for the roads and canals and other improvements so much needed by pioneers conquering the wilderness. In other words, everyone would benefit.

After the War of 1812, the Jeffersonian Republican party adopted this program. One of its loudest advocates was Senator Henry Clay, the Kentucky orator and a dashing political figure of the day. Clay had been one of the so-called Western "war hawks" who had helped to bring on the War of 1812. He had a large personal following in the West; he was greatly interested in Western development; and after the war he began to champion Hamilton's policy. A high protective tariff was passed in 1816, and Clay saw in this and in the rise of American industry the development of what he called the American System. Since large-scale financing was essential to the growth of such a system, a second Bank of the United States was created in 1816, vested with tight control over the nation's banking system.

What had happened then was that key principles of the old federalism — a high protective tariff, support of industry, creation of a national bank, the building of a wealthy and aristocratic class chained to the national government by self-interest — had crept quietly into the tent of the Republican party and had been adopted by federalism's former foes. While this was taking place

33

Henry Clay, famous Kentucky orator, was a major figure in American politics until his death in 1852. (PHOTO BY CUSHING)

on the highest levels of government, other forces were at work at the grass roots.

There was a strong, steady thrust toward a broader democracy. There was in the American people a deep-seated belief in those equal rights of man about which Jefferson had written in the Declaration of Independence. Thus the decade from 1820 to 1830 saw fierce battles in state after state to wipe out property qualifications for voters — to give the ballot to every man.

The wealthier classes fought hard against placing political power in the hands of "the mob." But in state after state old constitutions were scrapped and new ones adopted. Daniel Webster, the great Massachusetts orator, was horrified. "Power *naturally* and *necessarily* follows property," he thundered. In the New York convention, a conservative spokesman was shocked at the idea that "every man that works a day on the road, or serves an idle hour in the militia," should have just as much right to vote as the man who owned a factory. To the old Federalists, a man did not have much character or intelligence if he did not own property; the mere lack of possessions seemed to indicate that there was something wrong with him.

But the arguments of such conservatives fell on deaf ears. The people would not be denied, and before the end of the decade they had won the right to vote.

All of these changes began to force new political alignments and led to the development of what is sometimes called "the second party system." The first signs of this trend showed up in the Presidential election of 1824.

The candidates in that election called themselves Repub-

Daniel Webster, the famed Massachusetts orator. (PHOTO BY CUSHING)

licans, but some at heart believed as the old Federalists had believed. Foremost among these was John Quincy Adams, the son of John Adams and the Secretary of State under President Monroe. Of like mind was Henry Clay, spokesman for "the American System." Opposing this conservative faction within the Republican party was William H. Crawford of Georgia, Secretary of the Treasury and an old-line Jeffersonian. And then there was an unknown political entry, but one who was the people's hero — General Andrew Jackson of Tennessee, who was nicknamed "Old Hickory."

The election itself was quiet and far more orderly than later elections were to be. There was relatively little mudslinging. And, to a great degree, voting followed sectional lines.

Adams carried the New England states and got 26 of the 36 electoral votes of New York. But at the southern border of New York his drawing power stopped and Jackson's strength took over. The war hero swept the South and West, and he startled conservatives by carrying Pennsylvania and New Jersey. Crawford won only Virginia and his native Georgia; and Clay, with only a scattered following, wound up in fourth place. Jackson led Adams in the Electoral College vote by 99 to 84, but he did not have a majority. Again the election was thrown into the House of Representatives for a decision.

Here delegates voted by states. In order to win, a candidate had to have the votes of thirteen states. Jackson had eleven to start with; Adams, only seven. Crawford had suffered a stroke and had been eliminated, and so the contest narrowed down to just two men — Jackson and Adams. Clay held the balance of

John Quincy Adams, 6th U.S. President and son of John Adams. (PHOTO BY CUSHING)

An 1824 cartoon shows candidates Crawford, Adams, and Jackson toeing the mark for the White House race. At right, Clay scratches his head. (LIBRARY OF CONGRESS)

power; he controlled the votes of three states in the House. And so a deal was made — or so the Jacksonians always charged. Clay threw his votes to Adams in return for Adams's promise to make him Secretary of State. The deadlock was broken, and John Quincy Adams became President.

The Jacksonians shouted that they had been cheated. And indeed, there could be no doubt that the man desired by the majority of the people had been bilked in the horse trading in the

39

House. When Adams did in fact name Clay Secretary of State, he was accused of having won the Presidency by making a "corrupt bargain," and the acid-tongued John Randolph of Roanoke, Virginia, cried that it was a "combination unheard of till then, of the puritan and the blackleg."

Thus the election of 1824 had ended in bitterness and fury. And from that moment, the next campaign of 1828 began — and a new political lineup became inevitable.

Jacksonian Democracy

The Presidential election of 1828 was one of the dirtiest in American political history. It was also one of the most important, for it was the first in which the common people chose the President. And it also saw the formation of new parties.

The storm center of this upheaval was Andrew Jackson himself. He stood six feet one, ramrod straight. He was slender, weighing only about 140 pounds. The fiery red hair of his youth, a color that seemed to match his violent temper, had faded at sixty-one to a wiry gray. It receded from his high forehead and was tossed upward in a high plume, like the comb of a fighting cock. His face was long and narrow, his steel-blue eyes were intense in their deep sockets under hawklike brows.

Jackson was a man who had lived violently and hard. As a boy, his arm and face had been slashed when he had refused to clean a British officer's boots during the Revolution. As a young man, he had moved from North Carolina to Tennessee. He had become a leading lawyer in Nashville and had been noted for the temper that led him to fight duels and thrash opponents with his hickory stick. In 1791 he had married Rachel Donelson Robards, believing that her husband had divorced her. Two years later, however, it was discovered that there had actually been no divorce. Whereupon the vengeful husband, Lewis Robards, proceeded to divorce Rachel for living illegally with Jackson.

Although Jackson and Rachel got married again in 1794 after the divorce was final, the hero-general spent much of the rest of his life defending her honor. He was to have to defend it again in the campaign of 1828.

In this election there were only two candidates — John Quincy Adams and Andrew Jackson. The remnants of the old Federalist party and the conservative elements of the Republican party rallied around Adams, calling themselves National Republicans. Jackson's followers assumed the name of Democrats.

Once again, as in the days of Hamilton and Jefferson, the nation was polarized between two hostile faiths, each of which drew its strength from distinct voting classes. The conservative forces — the wealthy, the business and industrial barons, the social elite, the ministry, the press — massed behind the candidacy of Adams. Thus, the opposition to Jackson included two-thirds of the newspapers, four-fifths of the preachers, nearly all the manufacturers, and seven-eighths of the banking fraternity. On Jackson's side were "the people."

42

A portrait of Andrew Jackson, 7th President of the United States. (PHOTO BY CUSHING)

"The people" might have had second thoughts had they worshiped Jackson less as a hero and examined his career more critically. For there was little in his past to mark him as a zealous democrat and champion of the little fellow. In his earlier career in Congress he had supported Clay's American System; in Tennessee, he had sided with the landholding aristocracy against more humble, democratic elements. Jackson had been sympathetic to the growing Southern states' rights sentiment, but his record seemed to say he was more conservative than radical.

The election campaign did much to change and to radicalize Jackson. The National Republican press stooped to some of the foulest blows in history. It called Jackson's mother a "common prostitute" and his father a "mulatto man." It revived and spread the tangled story of Jackson's marriage and asked: "Ought a convicted adulteress and her paramour husband to be placed in the highest offices of this free and Christian land?"

The Jacksonian newspapers, what few there were of them, did their best to match the opposition's mudslinging. They accused Adams, the most upright of men, of being a crook and a gambler. They charged that he had lived with his wife before he got around to marrying her. They came up with the wild and preposterous story that Adams, while an envoy to Russia, had procured a beautiful American girl for the pleasure of Czar Alexander I. Revolted, Jackson wrote the editor of one such paper that published such filth: "I never war against females and it is only the base and cowardly that do."

When the votes were counted, it was clear that Andrew Jackson had won. Adams had been strong only in the New Eng-

This anti-Jackson cartoon of 1828 recalled Andrew Jackson's many executions of deserters from the army.
(NATIONAL ARCHIVES)

land states, the strongholds of the old Federalist party. He swept these six states, carrying four of them by margins of three to one or better. But Jackson was unbeatable in the South and the newer states of the West, and he carried by narrower margins the pivotal middle states of New York, New Jersey, and Pennsylvania.

Possibly more important than the election itself was the bitterness and hostility the campaign had left behind it. The nation was sharply divided between the powerful, the cultured, "the respectable" — and "the mob."

A portrait of Mrs. Andrew Jackson.
(PHOTO BY CUSHING)

The bitterness was most intense in the fierce heart of Andrew Jackson. His beloved wife, Rachel, had been shamed in the campaign; she had been so deeply wounded she would never recover. She had lived with Jackson in Washington when he was a congressman and a senator, and she enjoyed it. But she looked with horror at the prospect of becoming First Lady of a nation in which she had been made a figure of scandal. "I had rather be a doorkeeper in the house of God than to live in that palace in Washington," she wrote.

Rachel Jackson got her wish. She suffered a heart attack, and died on December 22, 1828.

Jackson, who had expressed his disgust at the personal attacks made upon President Adams, never forgave Adams or the men around him for their failure to disown or try to stop the slurs flung at Rachel. As he stood by her grave, tears streaming down his long gaunt face, he muttered fiercely: "Those vile wretches who have slandered her must look to God for mercy!"

In this vindictive mood, Andrew Jackson became the seventh President of the United States.

A crowd of small-town citizens greet President-elect Andrew Jackson as he journeys to Washington in 1829 for his inauguration. (PHOTO BY CUSHING)

The First Rift

There has never been another inauguration like that of Andrew Jackson. The people — or "the mob" as the followers of Adams regarded them — took over.

Long before the big day of March 4, 1829, the infant capital city on the Potomac began to swell to the bursting point with a horde of visitors. Daniel Webster wrote in amazement: "I have never seen such a crowd before. Persons have come five hundred miles to see General Jackson, and they really seem to think that the country has been rescued from some dreadful danger."

The President-elect tried to make the occasion a model of democratic simplicity. He rejected the idea of a grand parade. He had been staying at Gadsby's Tavern, and at the appointed hour, he left on foot, hickory stick in hand, and walked, bareheaded and erect, to the south terrace of the Capitol where he took the oath of office.

Then the new President mounted his horse and rode up Pennsylvania Avenue to the White House. The throngs that jammed every street and made the passage of vehicles impossible followed shouting and delirious at his heels. They did not halt at the White House gates, but surged inside in an irresistible tidal wave. They cheered and shouted, climbed up on chairs with their muddy boots, knocked over waiters to the accompanying crash of glass and china, and pinned Jackson himself into a corner, almost crushing him with their bodies. Women fainted, noses were bloodied. Finally, Jackson's closest followers made a flying wedge with their bodies, and the hero of the hour fled out a rear door of the White House, seeking safety in Gadsby's. The people quite literally had taken over "the people's house."

This "Democratic Revolution," as it was called, was to work many changes in American politics and also in the conduct of American political parties during the eight years of Jackson's two administrations. The first great change came with the adoption of the "spoils system," so called because of the old maxim "To the victor belong the spoils."

The mob of more than ten thousand persons who had descended on Washington had come not just to celebrate a victory but to feather their own nests. They wanted jobs. Their intention was to throw out the old job holders and replace them with true representatives of "the people."

In his earlier career Jackson had backed a civil service that would give security to federal employees; but now, as the leader of a new and hungry party, he listened to the clamor of his followers. Many servants of the old administration were fired from their jobs and their places taken by the new Jacksonians.

The crush at the White House after Andrew Jackson's inauguration. (THE
BETTMANN ARCHIVE)

The National Republican Press was soon filled with horror stories about suicides and starvation among the discharged federal workers. But the effects of the spoils system, though cruel, were greatly exaggerated. During Jackson's entire term in office, the purge affected no more than 20 percent of all federal officeholders.

Far more important was an issue that now came to the fore for the first time. This was the split between North and South. It was caused, not by slavery, but by the working of the protective tariff envisioned so long before by Hamilton as a means of encouraging Northern manufacturing.

The Congress of 1828 had enacted a new and exceptionally high tariff. It placed duties as high as 45 percent on manufactured goods imported from abroad. The South was hurt by this. Its livelihood depended upon the export of raw materials, especially cotton, but cotton prices were low as a result of overproduction. And the new tariff compelled the South to pay 45 percent more for manufactured goods than might have been the case had they been freely imported.

The financial squeeze brought South Carolina to the brink of rebellion. John C. Calhoun, that state's foremost political leader, had become Jackson's Vice-President in the election of 1828, but before that he had secretly authored a document known as the *South Carolina Exposition*. This argued that a single state might defy the federal government and its acts.

The Constitution was merely a compact among sovereign states, Calhoun declared. The 1828 tariff was "unconstitutional, unequal and oppressive." It made Southerners "the serfs of the

A portrait of John C. Calhoun. (CULVER PICTURES)

system." To remedy this injustice, he argued, any state had the
right to call a state convention, to declare such an act null and
void, and to refuse to be bound by it.

Southerners now rallied around this doctrine. It touched off
one of the great debates in Congress, with Daniel Webster clos-
ing one of his most famous orations with the words: "Liberty
and union, now and forever, one and inseparable!"

Where did Andrew Jackson stand in all of this? In his earlier career, he had backed the idea of states' rights. And when he had been elected, the South had expected he would favor its cause. But the South was to be disappointed. On April 13, 1830, both Jackson and Calhoun attended a dinner celebrating Jefferson's birthday. Twenty-four prearranged toasts were given, all favoring the Southern principle of states' rights. Then it came the President's turn.

Rising to his feet and staring directly at Calhoun with his piercing, eagle-eyed gaze, Jackson declared: "Our Federal Union. It must be preserved!"

One eyewitness noted that Calhoun was so shocked his hand shook and a bit of his drink spilled down the side of his glass. "An order to arrest Calhoun where he sat could not have come with more blinding, staggering force," he declared.

South Carolina was not to be stopped so easily, however. A state convention was called. It adopted an Ordinance of Nullification, declaring the tariff act void and threatening to leave the Union if efforts were made to enforce it.

Jackson acted forcefully. He strengthened the garrison at Fort Moultrie in Charleston Harbor. He sent seven revenue cutters and a warship to Charleston, all vessels ready for instant action. He also got Congress to pass an act, denounced by the South as the "Bloody Bill," giving him authority to use armed force to support the law.

War was avoided only by the passage of a more moderate tariff act. This was largely the work of John Quincy Adams, who had returned to Washington as a Massachusetts congressman.

Adams's new tariff greatly enlarged the list of free goods upon which no duties would be charged, and it cut tariffs on the protected list gradually so that they would be reduced to 20 percent by 1842.

This action deprived the South Carolina hotheads of the support of the rest of the South. But Jackson had made himself unpopular with many of the political leaders in that section. Calhoun resigned as Vice-President, and South Carolina refused to support Jackson in the election of 1832. It was the first small rift that was to lead to a new alignment of political parties — and ultimately to the Civil War.

The Whig Party

The Presidential election of 1832 brought important changes in political methods. For the first time, Presidential candidates were chosen at national party conventions and national platforms were drafted to spell out party stands on various issues.

Originally, Presidential candidates had been chosen by Congressional leaders of their parties in secret *caucuses*, or political meetings. Later the practice had grown up of having leaders of the state legislatures caucus (meet) and name their favorites. But the election of 1828 had begun to change all this. Once the common man in America had been given the right to vote, it followed almost inevitably that the selection of party candidates would soon be taken out of the hands of the few and placed in the hands of the many.

Oddly enough, this political change was brought about, not

Above, the purported drowning of William Morgan by members of the Masonic Fraternity, from an Anti-Mason almanac of 1830. Below, the cover of an Anti-Mason almanac, 1831. (THE BETTMAN ARCHIVE)

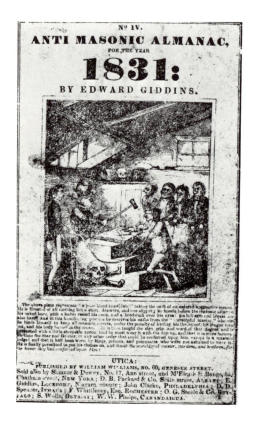

Nº IV.
ANTI MASONIC ALMANAC,
FOR THE YEAR
1831:
BY EDWARD GIDDINS.

The above plate represents "a poor blind candidate" taking the oath of an entered apprentice mason. He is divested of all clothing but a shirt, drawers, and one slipper; he kneels before the masonic altar on his naked knee, with a halter round his neck, and a hoodwink over his eyes: his left arm and breast are also bare, and in this humiliating posture he receives his oaths from the "worshipful master," who says he binds himself to keep all masonic secrets, under the penalty of having his throat cut, his tongue torn out, and his body buried in the ocean. He is then taught the sign, grip, and word of that degree, and is presented with a little sheepskin apron, told he must wear it with the flap up, and that it is more honorable than the Star and Garter, or any other order that could be conferred upon him, except in a masonic lodge; and that it had been worn by kings, princes, and potentates who were not ashamed to wear it. He is finally permitted to put his clothes on, and though the worshipful master, wardens, and brethren, for the honor they had conferred upon him!

UTICA:
PUBLISHED BY WILLIAM WILLIAMS, NO. 60, GENESEE STREET.
Sold also by Skinner & Dewey, No. 17, Ann street, and M'Elrath & Bangs, 82, Chatham street, NEW YORK; D. B. Packard & Co. State street, ALBANY; E. Giddins, LOCKPORT, Niagara county; John Clarke, PHILADELPHIA; D. D. Spencer, ITHACA; F Whittlesey, Esq. ROCHESTER; O. G. Steele & Co. BUFFALO; S. Wells, DETROIT; W. W. Phelps, CANANDAIGUA.

by a major party, but by a splinter group of no consequence that has been almost lost to history. This was the Anti-Masonic party, and it called the first national party convention on September 26, 1831. This party had grown out of a temporary frenzy of the political times. In 1826, a man named William Morgan of Batavia, New York, a former member of the secret society of Free and Accepted Masons, had announced his intention to publish a pamphlet revealing his Order's secrets. Shortly afterwards, Morgan was kidnapped and disappeared. It was widely believed he had been murdered.

The mystery sparked a wildfire reaction. In an increasingly democratic America, secret societies of all kinds were distrusted, and soon Anti-Masonry became a political issue in several states. President Jackson's enemies saw a chance to ride this gale of public passion and direct it to their own purposes. Men who were later to become prominent in the birth of the Republican party — William H. Seward and Thurlow Weed of New York, and Thaddeus Stevens of Pennsylvania — organized the Anti-Masons on a national basis. This party nominated William Wirt, a former attorney general, for the Presidency, but the Wirt candidacy never got anywhere. All the Anti-Masons really achieved was to set the style of holding national party nominating conventions.

The National Republican party was the first to imitate such measures. It met in Baltimore on December 12, 1831. There its members nominated Henry Clay and adopted a platform that denounced Andrew Jackson and all his works.

Clay's hatred of Jackson was deep, bitter, and vicious. He had wanted above all things to succeed John Quincy Adams as President at the end of Adams's second term; but there had been no second term for Adams, and thus no inheritance for Clay. Indeed, Jackson had hardly taken office, and had not had time to announce a single policy, before Clay began denouncing him as one of the greatest despots of all time.

When Adams, crushed by his defeat in 1828, abandoned the leadership of National Republicanism, Henry Clay seized the reins and labored to build an opposition party that would topple Jackson. He quickly became spokesman for the disgruntled and fearful political classes.

Jackson's renomination for a second term was inevitable, and it took place at the Democratic party's first national convention in Baltimore on May 21, 1832. So the battle lines were drawn between Jackson and Clay, with Clay needing a telling issue upon which to run.

At this point, hoping to further his candidacy, Clay raised a question that never should have been raised — the rechartering of the Bank of the United States. Although the bank bore the name of the American nation, it was in reality a privileged private institution. The federal government held only 20 percent of the stock and appointed but one-fifth of its board of directors. The bank, headed by Nicholas Biddle, had its headquarters in Philadelphia, and it handled all the government's banking business. Jackson regarded the bank as a dangerous monopoly, and he was convinced that it had used its influence against him in the campaign of 1828. But it seemed there was little he could do about it because the bank's charter did not expire until the year 1836.

Clay and Daniel Webster, however, persuaded Biddle to

apply for a recharter four years early. They argued that, with the 1832 election approaching, Jackson would not dare to veto a bill rechartering the bank. Biddle went along with the plan. And he used the bank's huge financial resources to buy influence. Newspaper editors who had formerly been hostile now received large and favorable loans — and suddenly changed their editorial tune. Congressmen also got favored treatment, with the bank extending their loans and being most generous to them so that, by 1831, fifty-nine of them were obligated to it.

With such powerful pressures behind it, the bank bill whipped through Congress on July 3, 1832. But on July 10 Andrew Jackson did what Clay and Webster had thought he would never dare to do; he vetoed the measure. The bank bill, Jackson said, would "make the rich richer and the potent more powerful." The Jacksonian press hailed his veto message as a "second Declaration of Independence." And the common people, on the whole, applauded his action.

The result was disastrous for Clay. Jackson once more swept the West, the Middle Atlantic states, and much of the South. Clay picked up only scattered electoral votes, and the Anti-Masons were ineffective. The final Electoral College count — Jackson, 219; Clay, 49; Wirt, 7.

Reelected, Jackson promptly moved to withdraw government deposits from the Bank of the United States and to place the money in sound state banks. His war against the bank brought on a severe depression. Jacksonians blamed the disaster on Biddle, whom they called "Nicholas I." As for the banking and business classes, they raged against "King Andrew I" and

59

One reaction to President Jackson's withdrawing support of the Bank of the United States was this cartoon. Nicholas ("Old Nick") Biddle (with devil's horns) is shown fleeing with reporters of various newspapers, as President Jackson brandishes his decision. Approving character at right is "Major Jack Downing," who symbolizes the people. (PHOTO BY CUSHING)

dictatorial Presidential powers. By late 1833, these anti-Jacksonians began to call themselves Whigs. They took the name from England's Whig party, which had stood for legislative supremacy against executive power. The leaders of the new American Whig party evidently hoped that the adoption of the name would rally independent, democratic Americans to their cause, united in their fear of a Presidential demon.

The new Whigs brought under their umbrella all who were "against" anything; their problem was uniting on a positive program. They could not decide what they were for.

The Whigs
and the Republicans

Most of the so-called "best" people were Whigs. The bankers who hated Jackson became Whigs. The manufacturers who wanted high protective tariffs were Whigs. The Anti-Masons and the antislavery followers of John Quincy Adams joined the Whig ranks. Henry Clay, with his Western following, brought many land-hungry Westerners into the party. In the South, plantation owners holding more than two-thirds of the slaves became Whigs. And in Virginia, North Carolina, even in Andrew Jackson's Tennessee, some old-line Jeffersonians, disturbed by Jackson's strong use of executive powers and fearing "executive tyranny," also turned Whig.

These were the leadership classes. They dominated business life in their localities; they set the tone of society. And they brought into the Whig party other influential groups — lawyers who represented business interests; preachers whose churches were supported by the well-to-do; teachers and professors; the literary elite of the day; shopkeepers, merchants, small businessmen, all who did business with business.

There was left to the Jacksonians only "the people," the rank-and-file of the poorer classes, the workingmen, the new immigrants, the small landowners. But, as always, there were more of these than there were of the prosperous.

The Whig problem from the beginning was that the party had gathered under one tent forces really hostile to each other — antislavery Northerners and Southern slave owners, for example. As a result, the party found it impossible to draft a workable platform. And in the election of 1836, it did not even dare to unite on a single candidate.

In fact, Jackson handpicked his successor, Vice-President Martin Van Buren, the wily politician who had built up the Democratic party in New York. The Whigs adopted the novel tactic of running three regional candidates, hoping to deny Van Buren a majority of the electoral votes and to throw the election into the House of Representatives. In New England, Daniel Webster carried the Whig banner; in Tennessee, there was Senator Hugh L. White, a former Democrat; in Pennsylvania and parts of the West, William Henry Harrison, a military hero of the Northwest Indian wars, became a candidate.

This three-way opposition was ineffective. Van Buren swept into office, scoring 170 electoral votes, 46 more than all of his opponents combined.

For the next four Presidential elections, the Whigs struggled to find a winning formula. The party was able to compete strongly with the Democrats in local and state contests, but it could never manage to bring its basically hostile factions together on a national program.

The Whigs discovered only one solution — to run "the hero." In 1840, although the party did not even draft a platform, it got its different wings together behind General William Henry Harrison, the "Tippecanoe" of Indian fighting fame. Helped by the catchy war cry, "Tippecanoe and Tyler Too" (the Tyler was John Tyler of Virginia, the Vice-Presidential candidate), the Whigs managed to shunt the issues and still defeat Van Buren. In 1848, the same formula worked for them again as they elected General Zachary Taylor, a hero of the Mexican War.

Unfortunately for the Whigs, both of these hero-general-Presidents died shortly after they took office, and the administrations they had been elected to head fell apart. As a result, from the election of Jackson in 1828 until 1860, the Democratic party was the actual party of power and the party upon which the peace and welfare of the nation largely depended.

Despite its power, however, the events of the 1850's began to tear the Democratic party apart and shift its members' loyalties. The Democratic following in the South was made up largely of poor whites and small landowners. These were classes that owned few slaves or could not afford slaves at all. Yet, strangely enough, these were the very groups that were most aroused by the slavery question.

While the poorer Southerners might lead miserable lives and were often worse off than the slaves themselves, they were at

*Whig campaign banner showing
Vice-Presidential candidate Millard Fillmore,
who succeeded Taylor. Taylor died
after one year and four months in office.*
(PHOTO BY CUSHING)

least white and free. Hence, Northern Abolitionist talk about freeing the slaves threatened their only claim to status. For this reason, they were wild to defend their region's "peculiar institution," regardless of the fact that they themselves enjoyed none of its advantages.

Yet, in a different way, the slavery issue was playing hob with the Whig party. The Whigs' great congressional leaders Henry Clay and Daniel Webster had worked out compromise after compromise to avoid civil war and to save the union. But by the mid-1850's, Clay and Webster were gone, the slavery question waxed hotter than ever, and there was no strong congressional leadership to dampen the fires.

The boiling point was reached in the fierce struggle over the fate of new territories stretching clear to the Pacific which had been opened up for settlement after the Mexican War of 1846–47. The South wanted the right to introduce slavery into the new territories at will. The North, however, wanted slavery banned. On this issue, both of the established parties began to split apart.

The Whigs were the first to break up, change, and regroup. The mid-1850's were a time of turmoil in politics. A multitude of political groups sprang up. There was the Free Soil party, the Barnburners, women's suffrage and temperance movements, and — most powerful of all — the so-called Know-Nothings. This was a party based on outright hatred — hatred of immigrants and Catholics. Members were initiated with great secrecy and swore never to reveal the "mysteries" of the organization. Out-

A cartoon entitled "The Presidential Fishing Party of 1848." (CULVER PICTURES)

The "Know-Nothings" accused German and Irish immigrants of stealing American elections and wielding the power behind big city political machines.
(LIBRARY OF CONGRESS)

siders attempting to obtain information were told "I know nothing about it." As a result, the organization was dubbed the Know-Nothing party. In the frenzy of the times, the Know-Nothings swept state after state in the mid-term 1854 election, and it appeared to many that they would capture the Presidency in 1856.

In this broil of new movements, the Whigs practically fell apart. The 1854 mid-term elections showed they were no longer a force. And so, soon afterward, like so many brush fires breaking out in a tinder-dry season, spontaneous conventions were held in many parts of the North, with the aim of forming a new party. Whigs, antislavery Democrats, and Free Soilers gathered at Ripon, Wisconsin, in one of the first of these sessions, and resolved "to throw old party organizations to the winds and organize a new party on the sole basis of the non-extension of slavery." These Ripon delegates and others in various states began to call themselves Republicans.

Here was a political development that was different and surprising. In the past, new political parties had always been formed from elements that were fiercely opposed to the forces in power on some basic issue. Before, party formation had always been aided by the appeal of certain commanding personal leaders — Washington and Hamilton for the Federalists; Jefferson for the original Republicans; Jackson for the Democrats; Clay for the Whigs. But this time there was no leader about whom to rally. The new Republican party was being born on a wave of grass-roots sentiment.

While it may seem strange today — when modern Republicans are noted for their general conservatism — these Republicans were forming a radical and a sectional party. They championed the workingman. They called for free homesteads in the undeveloped West. They were fiercely opposed to the extension of slavery. They were for "reform" of every kind. And so they brought together under one banner all the opposition movements of their day.

But the new Republican party was not split as the old Whigs had been split — between Northern and Southern wings. The new party was a party of the North, of states stretching from New England across the broad northern reaches of America to Wisconsin. In this compactness lay the party's strength; and, in this representation of one section of the nation pitted against another lay the seeds of future civil war.

The new Republican party was first tested in the Presidential election of 1856. Having no single national leader, the Republicans tried the old Whig tactic of running a hero — General

*"Free Speech, Free Soil, Free
Men — and Fremont!"
This was the campaign slogan of the
new Republican party in 1856.
Their ticket featured the dashing
General John C. Frémont who, at forty-three,
was the youngest-looking man yet to
run for the Presidency.
But Frémont ultimately lost to Democrat
James P. Buchanan.* (PHOTO BY CUSHING)

John C. Frémont, a dashing figure known as "The Pathfinder of
the Rockies." A future President, Abraham Lincoln of Illinois,
campaigned for Frémont, but he disliked the radical, abolitionist
elements in the party so much that he refused even to use the
name Republican. Although Frémont lost to Democrat James P.
Buchanan, the new party showed amazing strength, polling
nearly 1.4 million votes. It was to be the last Presidential victory
for the Democrats for a long, long time.

The Democratic party, like the nation itself, was becoming
divided over the slavery issue. Stephen A. Douglas of Illinois,
nicknamed the "Little Giant," leader of the Northern Democrats,
tried to find some basis for compromise. In the spring of 1860,
when his party met in convention at Charleston, South Carolina,
he did his best to skirt the slavery issue by drafting a platform
saying the question should be left to the courts to decide. South-

Stephen A. Douglas, the "Little Giant,"
who was Lincoln's opponent in
a famous series of debates
before the Civil War. (PHOTO BY CUSHING)

ern Democrats wanted a flat declaration that neither Congress nor the courts could interfere with slavery in the territories.

Douglas and his followers realized that such a stand would be political disaster. They refused. Hate boiled over. Northern Democrats almost came to blows with Southern Democrats, and the Southerners walked out of the convention, tearing the party apart.

The Northern wing of the party met later in Baltimore and nominated Douglas. The Southerners held their own convention and nominated Vice-President John C. Breckenridge of Kentucky.

69

Still another Southern faction — a group composed largely of those great planters who had been former Whigs — formed the Constitutional Union party and put John Bell of Tennessee into the race.

With the opposition riding off in all directions, the Republicans gathered in Chicago and picked for their candidate one of the truly great figures in American history — Abraham Lincoln. Tall and gawky, with sad deep-set eyes, Lincoln was a truly towering figure, a man of far vision and deep, compassionate understanding. Born in a log cabin, largely self-educated, he was known as "the rail splitter from Illinois" and "Honest Abe." He had the gift of eloquence. He could write memorable English prose — as he was later to do in the Gettysburg Address— that lives today; and on the public platform, he spoke without flourishes but with a sincerity and directness that reached the hearts of his audiences. When Lincoln was nominated by the Republicans, he possessed two strong convictions: he believed that the slavery issue could no longer be dodged or compromised, that it must be faced and settled; and he was determined, in the face of Southern threats of secession, to preserve the Union.

The campaign of 1860 was waged in an atmosphere of hate. In Congress, Northern and Southern senators and representatives walked to their desks — armed. In the galleries, their followers watched their fierce debates — also armed. The South considered Lincoln and his so-called Black Republicans as enemies from a foreign land, and Southern fire-eaters threatened to leave the Union should Lincoln be elected.

Douglas became alarmed at the gathering crisis. He toured

70

A portrait of Abraham Lincoln, the Republican candidate who became the 16th President of the United States. (PHOTO BY CUSHING)

the South and declared that if he were elected he would deal with any threat of secession just as Old Hickory had in the nullification furor of 1828. But now no words, no threats could prevent catastrophe.

When the votes were counted, the nation had divided tragically along sectional lines. Lincoln swept the North and the new Western states of Oregon and California. Breckenridge car-

71

ried the South; Bell, the border states; Douglas, only Missouri and parts of New Jersey. Lincoln had only 40 percent of the popular vote, but he had carried the North so solidly that he rolled up 180 electoral votes to 72 for Breckenridge, his closest rival.

The Black Republicans had won. Neither the North nor South was now in the mood for the kind of compromise that had saved the Union previously. And the Civil War followed — the most tragic conflict in our history, for it pitted American against American.

The Enduring Parties

From the Civil War until the present day, the two great enduring parties have been the Republican and the Democratic. They have not always remained the same parties in principles or in strength. Both have undergone many changes.

The Civil War made the Republican party the dominant party of the nation for more than seventy years — from 1860 to 1932. It was the party that had saved the Union. The Democrats, on the other hand, had been tainted by their Southern connections. In the campaign of 1864, the Democrats had opposed Lincoln, arguing that the war was a failure when, in fact, it was on the verge of being won. If this had not been treason, it had been folly, and for generations that party was discredited in the minds of many Americans.

Through large sections of the nation, particularly in the

73

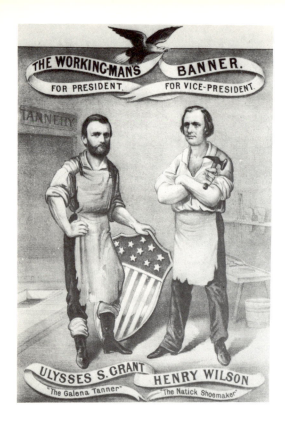

A Republican party campaign poster for the Presidential election of 1868. Ulysses S. Grant won and spent two terms in office. (PHOTO BY CUSHING)

farm belt and rural areas, one was born into Republicanism. It was a faith no more to be questioned than the religious beliefs one acquired in Sunday School. But for the Democrats, in election after election, the cause was almost hopeless.

Only the South remained solidly Democratic. The war and the evils of the postwar Reconstruction period resulted in generations of Southerners being virtually born into a political faith — in this instance, into the Democratic party. The South became, and has remained almost until the present time, virtually a one-party area where a victory in the Democratic primary assured election in the fall — sometimes without even opposition.

First appearance of the elephant as the symbol of the Republican party was in this cartoon by Thomas Nast in Harper's Weekly, November 7, 1874. It is shown being stampeded by lesser political animals into a pit labeled "Southern Claims and Chaos." (PHOTO BY CUSHING)

This inequality of power had its effect on both parties. The Republican party had begun as a radical party. In its first campaigns, it had even displayed Jefferson's picture on its posters, claiming it had inherited his ideals. But the longer the party held unchallenged power, the more conservative it became. Not Jefferson, but Hamilton, became its idol. Increasingly, its interests became not those of the common man but of the big businesses that were changing the face of America. Indeed, it became so wedded to business that it adopted ever higher protective tariffs, sometimes raising the rates to such levels that they strangled international trade and brought on depressions.

The control of the Republican party by the classes of business and wealth was never more obvious than in the election of 1896. William McKinley, a staunch Ohio conservative, was promoted into the White House by a mastermind of big business, Mark Hanna, a multimillionaire industrial baron.

During this period the Democratic party — from the end of the Civil War to the early 1900's — floundered helplessly, burdened by the past and at loss for a following. It flirted with the tariff issue; it tried to pose as the party of everyman. But its leadership was for the most part as conservative as the Republican, and this did it no good. It did not make the party any better loved by business nor did it woo the common people. The Democrats remained a minority party, strong only in the South and in pockets in the North, where boss-ridden political machines sometimes captured power in such great cities as New York.

Although the leaders of both major parties had their heads buried in the sand like an ostrich, change was coming. It was coming because conditions in the nation were forcing it; and, if the major parties would not listen, then a rebellion in the ranks of the people would ultimately force them to see and to heed.

The 1890's were a disaster period on the farms. With the Republicans giving capitalism a highly protected market, prices on manufactured articles soared. But the farmer had no such protection. The prices on farm produce dropped, and millions of Americans who lived on the farms were caught in a two-way squeeze, much as the South had been in 1828: they had to pay more for the articles they purchased, and they received less for those they sold.

By 1893 it cost farmers in the West more to raise crops than they could get from their sale. Corn dropped to 8 cents a bushel, oats to 10; beef brought 2 cents a pound; and butter and eggs simply could not be sold. Farmers in desperation mortgaged their properties — and at 10 percent interest rates, at that, to protected Eastern money men. When the panic of 1893 struck, more than 11,000 farm mortgages had been foreclosed in Kansas alone, and two years later it was estimated that, in fifteen counties of that state, loan companies owned from 75 to 90 percent of the land.

"Raise less corn and more hell," agitators began to tell the farmers — and the farmers listened.

In 1892 a number of farm organizations gathered in Omaha and founded the People's party — or, as it came to be known, the Populist party. They denounced both major parties as the pawns of Wall Street. They called for the free coinage of silver, a graduated income tax to make the wealthy pay their proper share of the costs of government, a shorter work week for urban laborers (work hours were then almost unlimited), and the popular election of United States senators, then chosen by the senates of the various state legislatures.

With this program, the Populists shocked the older parties by the vote they rolled up for their little-known Presidential candidate, James B. Weaver of Iowa. They polled over a million popular votes in 1892, and Weaver captured twenty-two votes in the Electoral College, the first time since the birth of the Republican party that such a thing had happened.

The need for political change was obvious, but the Repub-

The Greenback party's platform, a political cartoon of 1879. (THE BETT-MANN ARCHIVE)

licans, married to the big-money interests of the East and Midwest, could not change. Only the Democrats could. And, in the elections of 1896 and 1900, they tried.

William Jennings Bryan, a matchless young orator, came virtually out of nowhere at the Democratic convention in 1896, and with an impassioned speech in which he cried that the nation was being impaled on "a cross of gold," he stampeded the delegates. He and the Western forces that he led wrested control of the party machinery from Eastern conservative Democrats, and in the campaign that followed, the rebellious Populists merged with the Democratic party.

Bryan's great outcry, appealing to the West, horrifying to

78

the moneyed interests of the nation, was for "free silver." Earlier, in 1873, Congress had passed an act which omitted silver from the list of coins authorized for domestic use. Silver was in scarce supply at the time, and the ban did not seem to matter. But shortly afterward, great new silver mines were discovered and opened up in the West, and at the same time the supply of gold began to dwindle. "Tight" money (those 10 percent interest rates) helped to make paupers out of Western farmers, and so there was a great outcry for "free silver" — and a larger, cheaper supply of money.

"Free silver" was only one plank of Bryan's platform, however. He wore himself hoarse in nationwide speechmaking, calling for the regulation of the railroads, for government restraint of trusts and the great economic powers that he saw as grinding down the common man, the laborer, the farmer. He was, he roared, trying to save the people from "the most merciless and unscrupulous gang of speculators on earth — the money power."

Bryan shocked and horrified the leading classes in American society. Big business fought him with a scare campaign, threatening workers with the specter of an economic depression and lost jobs if Bryan won. It worked, and Bryan lost to McKinley in the elections of 1896 and 1900.

Oddly enough, however, Bryan in defeat soon began to win victories. When President McKinley was assassinated in 1901, Vice-President Theodore Roosevelt came to power. And Roosevelt was a far different kind of man.

He could not be controlled. The conservative forces in charge of the Republican party had known this and had virtu-

A portrait of William Jennings Bryan.
His famous "cross of gold" speech
in favor of "free silver" at
the Democratic convention of 1896
won him the party's nomination
for President when he was
only thirty-six.
(PHOTO BY CUSHING)

ally forced the Vice-Presidential nomination on him, intending to "bury" him in this office where he would have no influence and could thus be forgotten. Then, to their horror, McKinley was killed, and that "wild man," as some called him, was in the White House.

Although Roosevelt had a strong conservative streak in him, he also had a sensitive ear for the needs of his time. It was not long before he began to adopt as his own key elements of the programs advocated by Bryan and the Populists. He launched a campaign to break up the great trusts that were establishing virtual monopolies over vast areas of American business life. He got Congress to pass a Pure Food and Drug Act, protecting consumers against contaminated foods. He welcomed labor leaders

80

*A political cartoon of 1896
depicts William Jennings Bryan as
"the boy ... standing on the burning deck,
whence all but him have fled."
Note that the "deck" is
the defeated "free silver" platform.*
(CULVER PICTURES)

to the White House. He began a conservation campaign, preserving for the government and the people great areas of timberland and water resources that greedy interests were eager to loot.

When Roosevelt left the Presidency in 1909, he had given the Republican party, for the first time since its founding, a liberal and progressive image. It was not to last, however. Once that "wild man" had gone off to Africa to hunt lions, the old special interests found their way back into the saddle. Roaring in anger at the betrayal of his programs, Roosevelt returned in 1912, seeking his party's nomination for the Presidency against William Howard Taft, the man who had succeeded him.

But the conservatively controlled Republican party wanted no part of its former president. Taft was nominated, and Roose-

Kemble's cartoon of 1912 depicts the demise of Theodore Roosevelt's hastily formed "Bull Moose" party. (PHOTO BY CUSHING)

velt bolted, becoming the candidate of a hastily formed Progressive, or "Bull Moose," party. His personal appeal to all classes of voters was so great that he split the Republican vote in the general election, and the Democratic candidate, Woodrow Wilson, former president of Princeton University and Governor of New Jersey, stole into the White House as a minority President.

Wilson adopted the slogan of the "New Freedom" for his administration, and he took up and rammed through Congress many of the liberal programs originally proposed by the Populists. The graduated income tax was adopted; the high protective tariff was slashed for the first time since 1857; the banking system was reorganized; acts were passed to curb unfair business

82

practices; the farmers and labor were encouraged, helped, and protected.

World War I put an end to Wilson's reforms, and public reaction to the war and hard times restored the Republicans to power in the election of 1920. There followed twelve years of Republican rule under some of the most conservative administrations the nation has ever seen. Once more the old familiar cycle was repeated. Income taxes were slashed for the wealthy. Ruinously high protective tariffs practically strangled foreign trade. After the disastrous failure of the stock market in 1929, a depression such as the nation had never seen hit the farms and soon spread to the entire country in a horror that seemed to have no end.

The Great Depression of the 1930's changed the political complexion of America. The Republican party, since the Civil War the majority party, now became the minority party. The Democrats, taking advantage of the times, found themselves a great political leader, Franklin D. Roosevelt, Governor of New York.

Although he was crippled by polio, Roosevelt was a man of matchless faith and courage. When he took office in March, 1933, most of the banks in the nation had collapsed and were closed. In some states, not a single bank was open, and even police, teachers, and firemen were being "paid" in paper scrip issued by their municipalities — paper promises to pay later if and when money became available. The nation was in despair. In the farm states, farmers sat by their doors with loaded shotguns, determined not to be driven off their lands by creditors foreclosing mortgages. Roosevelt, in his inaugural address, rallied the nation. "The only thing we have to fear is fear itself," he asserted — and the people listened and took heart.

Roosevelt called his program the New Deal, and in the most active hundred days in American political history, he drove through Congress reform after reform. Bank deposits were guaranteed by the federal government, and the banks reopened. Wall Street speculation, which had run wild and had helped to bring on the depression, was curbed, and standards of worth and honesty were set for stock issues. Farmers were aided with loans and measures to protect prices. Labor unions, crippled by restrictive laws, were given the freedom to bargain with employers. Such programs, in the tradition of Jefferson and Jackson, favored the run-of-the-mill people of the nation against the pressures and powers of special interests. And Roosevelt, for securing their passage, was hated and vilified by many, just as Jefferson and Jackson had been before him.

"That man," conservatives called him with hate and scorn, but "that man" was a master politician. He built a political power complex that was to be unbeatable for twenty years. It was based upon the solid Democratic South, the votes of labor, and the support of ethnic voting blocs — the Jews, Catholics, descendants of foreign-born minority groups — in the great cities where Democratic machines were most powerful.

After twenty years of Democratic rule, the Republicans returned to power in 1952, using the old Whig tactic of running "the hero." He was General Dwight D. Eisenhower, the great commander of World War II in Europe, and it was "Ike's" flash-

*Franklin Delano Roosevelt, 31st President of the United States, broadcasts
to the nation from the Oval Room of the White House in 1936.*

ing grin and warm personality that carried his party to power. His was a personal, not a party, victory. But there were signs, even in the 1950's, that a changed political lineup was coming.

The Solid South was no longer solid for the Democrats. Eisenhower broke through, carrying a number of Southern states. The reason was to be found not only in the famous Eisenhower charm but in the stands that had earlier been taken by the national Democratic party. The party under President Harry S. Truman had begun to champion the Negro's demand for equal rights and opportunities; but the Democratic party in the South since the Civil War had been a party of white racism, devoted to passing laws that would keep the Negro from voting, that would keep him "in his place," technically free but actually almost a slave.

As the nation entered the 1970's, old political loyalties were changing. The Republican party of President Richard M. Nixon was trying to build a new national majority through a "Southern strategy" that appealed to white racism combined with the old rural Republicanism and an appeal to those working and middle classes that felt threatened by the rise of the Negro and racial disturbances. The Democrats were struggling to hold together their old labor following and the ethnic and Negro voters in the cities of the North and Midwest. No one could tell whether the Republicans' hoped-for new majority would jell or whether the Democrats could keep enough of the old Roosevelt coalition to remain the nation's major party. But one thing was certain: it was a new, a different political ball game.

Index

Republican party, Jeffersonian (*see* Jeffersonian Republican party)
Republican party, National (*see* National Republican party)
Revolution, American, 2, 4, 16, 17, 21, 22, 23, 28
"Revolution of 1828," 49
Ripon, Wisconsin, 66
Robards, Lewis, 42
Robards, Rachel Donelson (*see* Jackson, Rachel)
Roosevelt, Franklin D., 83-84, 86
Roosevelt, Theodore, 79-82
Rutland Herald, 27

Scourge of the Aristocracy, The, 27
Secession, threats of (and Lincoln), 70
Sedition Act, 26-29
Senate, Jay treaty debate in, 23
Senators, popular election of, 77
Seward, William H., 57
Slavery issue of 1850's, 63-72
Slaves, owners of (*see* Plantation owners)
"Solid South," 74, 76, 84, 86
South Carolina and tariff issue, 51-54
South Carolina Exposition, 51-52
Southern Democrats (1860), 68-72
"Southern strategy" (Nixon's), 86
Speech, freedom of, 26-29
"Spoils system," 49-51
State, Secretary of, 2, 7, 37, 39-40
States' rights doctrine, 44, 51-52
Stevens, Thaddeus, 57
Stock market:
    crash of (1929), 83
    regulation of, 84

Taft, William Howard, 81
Tammany, Sons of, 17
Tariff, protective (*see* Protective tariff)

Taylor, John, 17
Taylor, Zachary, 63
Temperance movement (1850's), 65
Territories of the U.S., slavery issue in, 65-66
"Tight" money, 79
"Tippecanoe and Tyler Too," 63
Tories, 4, 9
Trade (U.S.), British and, 22, 23
Treasury, Secretary of, 2, 6-8, 37
Truman, Harry S., 86
Trusts, regulation of, 79
    (*See also* Big business)
Tyler, John, 63

Van Buren, Martin, 62, 63
Voting:
    decline in (1819), 32
    property qualifications and, 14, 35, 55

War of 1812:
    Federalist party during, 31-32
    political results of, 32-35
Washington, George, 4, 19, 25, 67
    and Hamilton-Jefferson conflict and, 1-2, 5, 6-8, 13
Weaver, James B., 77
Webster, Daniel, 35, 48, 52, 62, 64
    and Bank of the U.S. (2nd), 58-59
Weed, Thurlow, 57
Whig party, 60-67, 70, 84
Whigs (in Revolution), 4
White, Senator Hugh L., 62
Wilson, Woodrow, 82-83
Wirt, William, 57, 59
Women's suffrage movement (1850's), 65
World War I, 83

Yorktown, Battle of, 2